All About Me

Point and Say

All About Me
a very first picture book

LORENZ BOOKS

This edition first published in 1998 by Lorenz Books

© Anness Publishing Limited 1998

Lorenz Books is an imprint of
Anness Publishing Limited
Hermes House
88-89 Blackfriars Road
London SE1 8HA

ISBN 1 85967 799 1

A CIP catalogue record for this book is available from the British Library

Publisher: Joanna Lorenz
Senior Editor: Catherine Barry
Designer: Julie Francis

Printed in Hong Kong/China

1 3 5 7 9 10 8 6 4 2

Contents

My Body

My Day

My Home

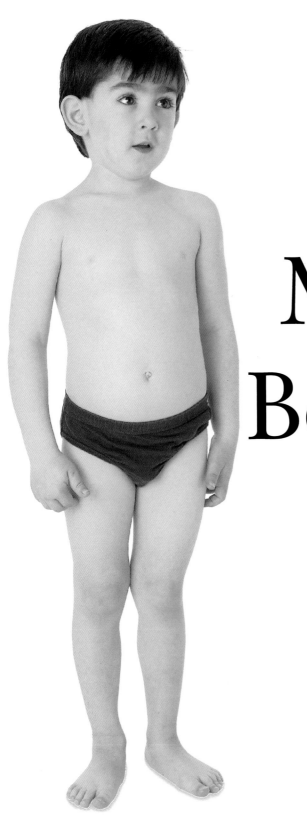

My Body

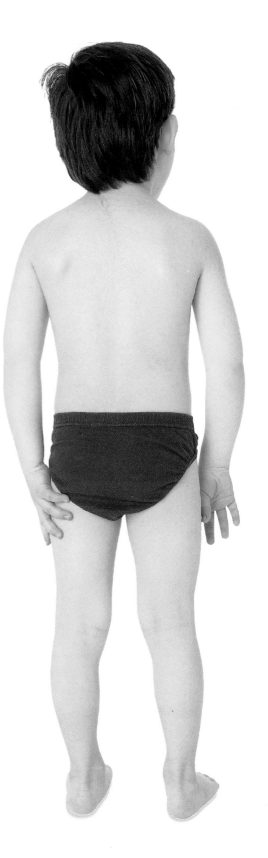

Body

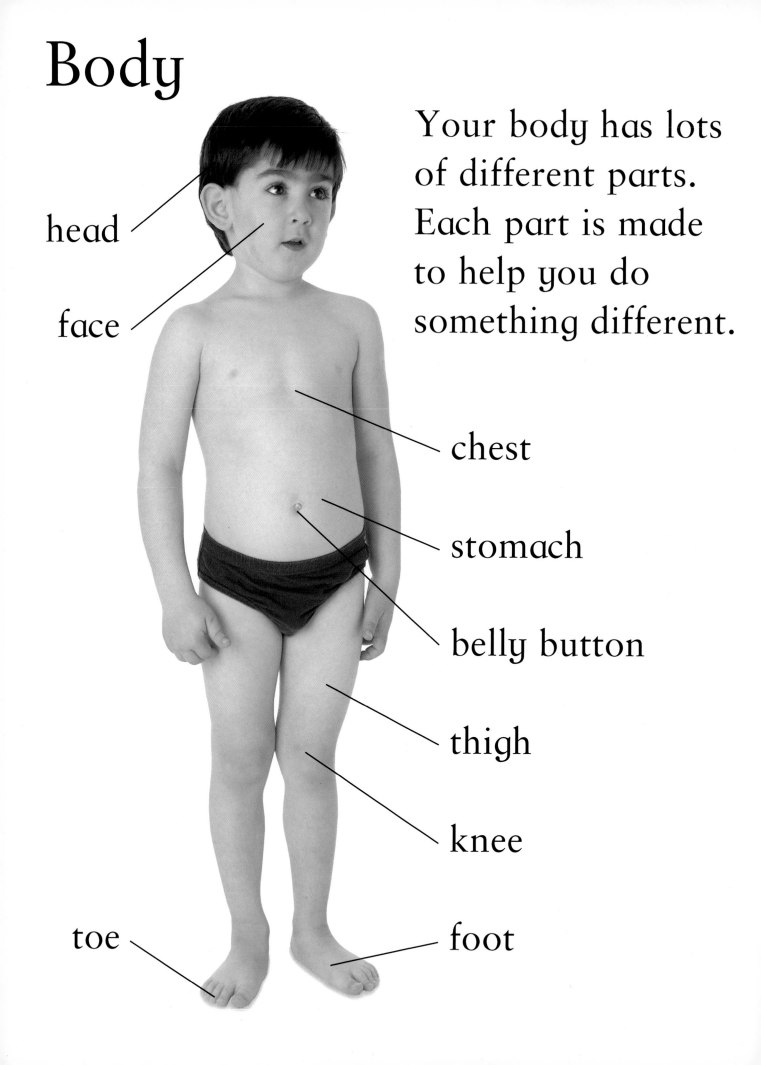

Your body has lots of different parts. Each part is made to help you do something different.

head

face

chest

stomach

belly button

thigh

knee

toe

foot

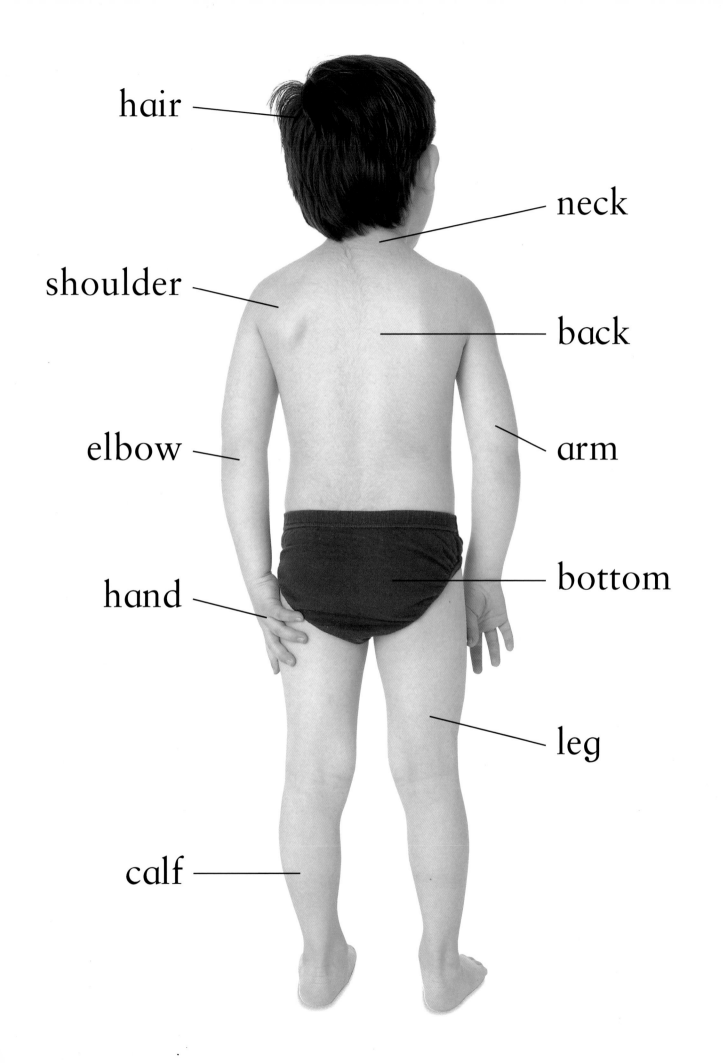

hair

neck

shoulder

back

elbow

arm

hand

bottom

leg

calf

Skin and Bones

Your body is covered in skin. Inside your body are bones. Your bones are joined together to make your skeleton.

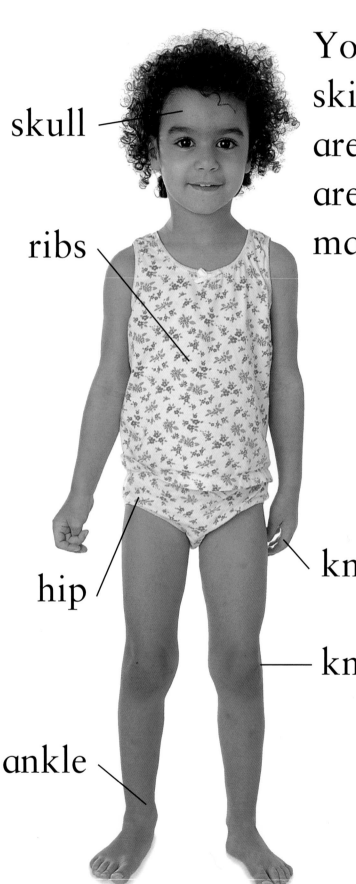

skull

ribs

hip

ankle

knuckles

kneecap

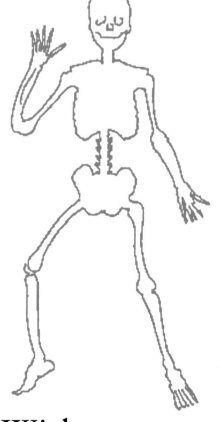

Without your skeleton, you would be a big blob!

See if you can feel these bones. Press hard!

wrist   elbow   knee

Skin can be dark... light... or freckly.

Mouth

Your mouth is for talking, eating and smiling!

You move your tongue and lips to talk.

lips

teeth

tongue

You use your teeth to take a bite of food.

You use your tongue to taste your food.

You use your mouth to...

smile

blow up a balloon

After chewing your food, you swallow it.

blow bubbles

lick an ice cream

Eyes

You use your eyes to see all around you. When you are sad or hurt, tears fall from your eyes.

eyebrow

pupil

eyelid

eyelashes

eye

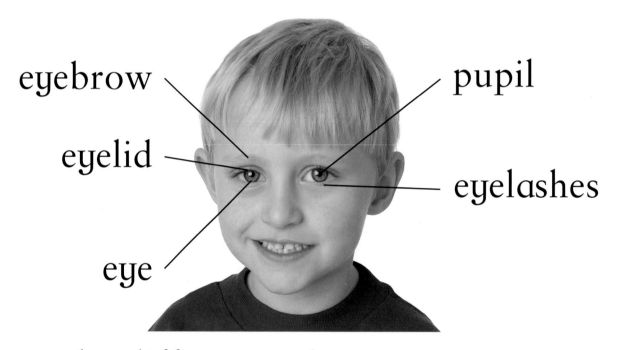

Eyes can be different colours. What colour are your eyes?

blue eyes

brown eyes

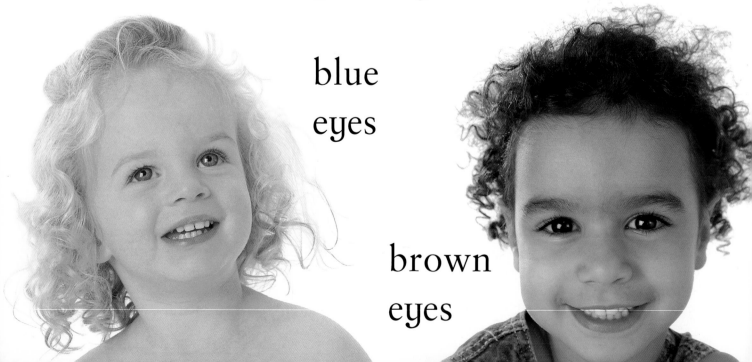

You use
your eyes
to read.

Sunglasses
help us to
see in
bright
sunshine.

Glasses help eyes
to see better. Do
you wear glasses?

Can you
see my
eyes?

Nose

You use your nose to smell things. You sneeze through your nose, too.

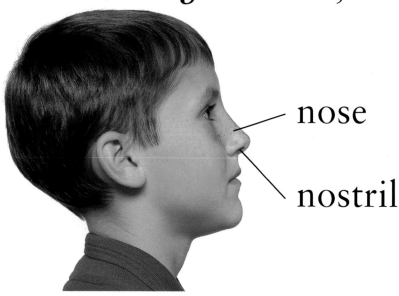

nose

nostril

A-choo! Sometimes, sneezing means that you have a cold.

Flowers smell good.

When you have a cold, you blow your nose.

These animals use their noses to help them find food.

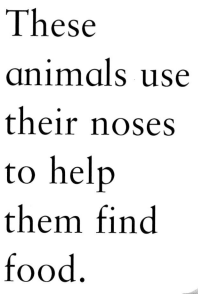
dog

pig

cat

Do these things smell good or bad?

pasta

herbs

onion

rose

perfume

Ears

You use your ears to hear all the noises around you.

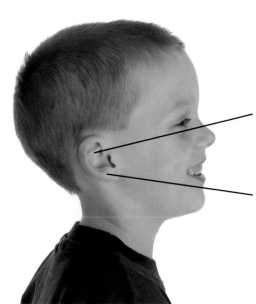

ear

earlobe

What noises do these things make?

drum

bells

clapping

baby crying

cassette player

You use your ears to listen to stories...

and to music...

or to hear whispers.

Some people use a hearing aid to help their ears work better.

I'm shouting. Can you hear me?

earrings earmuffs

Hair

Hair grows on your body.

curly hair

short hair

long hair

straight hair

Hair can be different colours.

blonde hair

brown hair

black hair

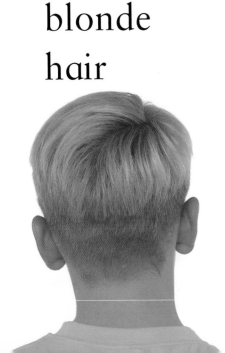

You need to
brush your
hair...

or comb it...

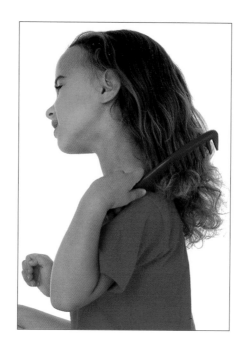

and have
it cut.

Babies do not
have much hair.

Your skin
is covered with
tiny hairs.

Hands

You use your hands to hold, feel and make things.

finger

knuckle

palm

thumb

nail

wrist

Do you draw with your left hand or your right hand?

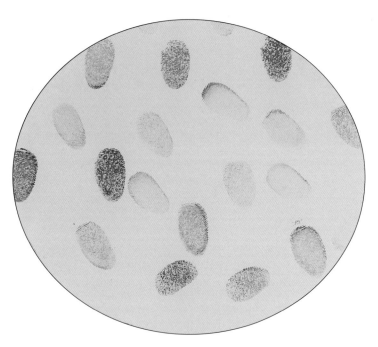

Everybody has different fingerprints. What are yours like?

Look at all
these things
your hands
help you do.
Can you
think of
some more?

making
music

catching

painting

cutting

cooking

Arms and Legs

Your arms and legs help you to walk,
run, jump, dance and play games.

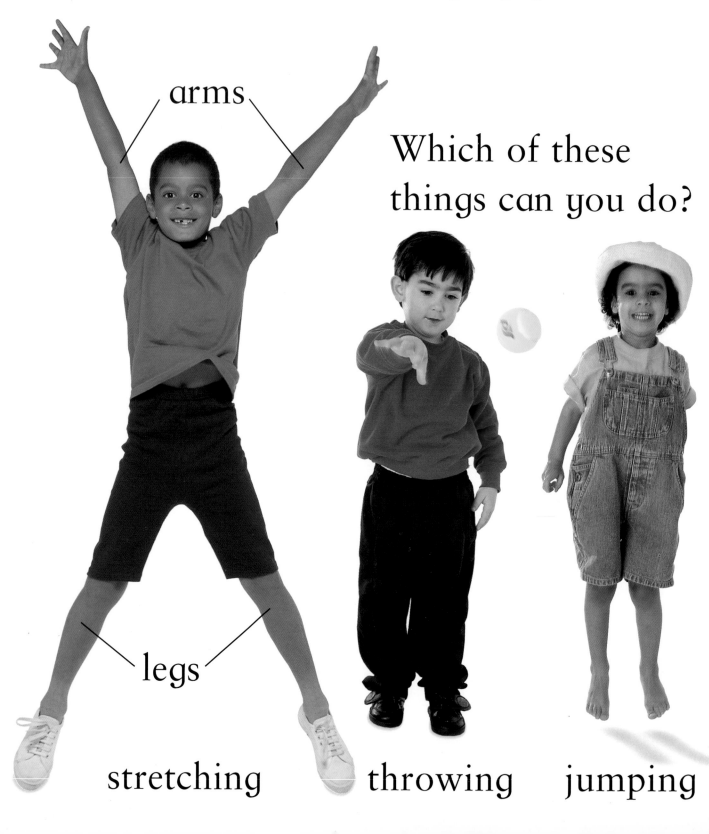

arms

Which of these
things can you do?

legs

stretching   throwing   jumping

dancing

cycling

standing
on one
leg

skipping

hopping

Faces

Faces show how we are feeling.

I feel very sleepy.

I feel very angry.
I am frowning.

I feel happy.
I am smiling.

I am
laughing
and feel
happy.

I feel upset.
I am crying.

I feel very sad.
I might cry.

Babies

Babies grow up into adults.

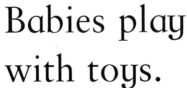

Babies play with toys.

They drink milk.

They sleep in cots until they are bigger.

Babies wear
nappies.

They wear
small clothes.

They need
lots of food
to grow.

Growing

Baby clothes
are very small.

You grow too big
for your clothes.

Little boys grow
into big boys.

fingernails

toenails

Your nails grow, too. They have to be cut quite often.

Little girls grow into bigger girls.

Growing Up

Babies grow up into children.

babies

children

Children grow up into teenagers.

Teenagers grow up into adults.

Can you name these parts of the body?

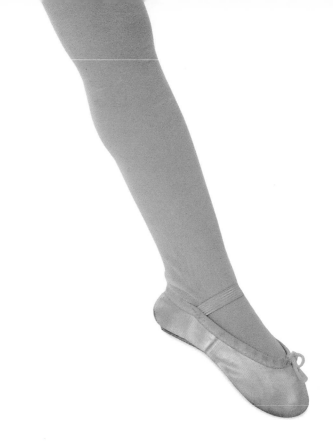

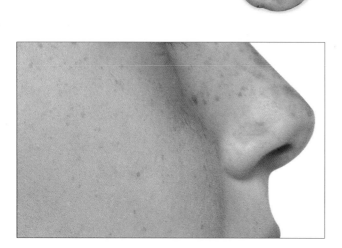

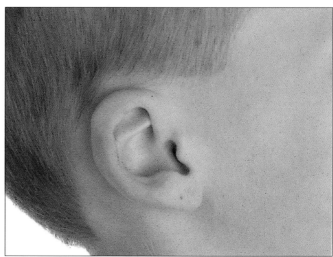

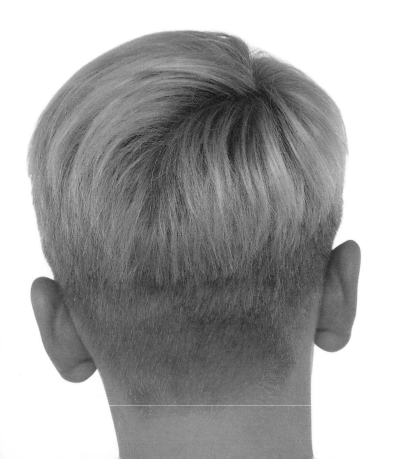

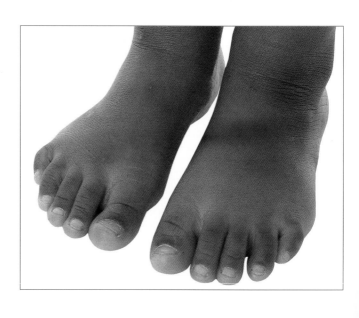

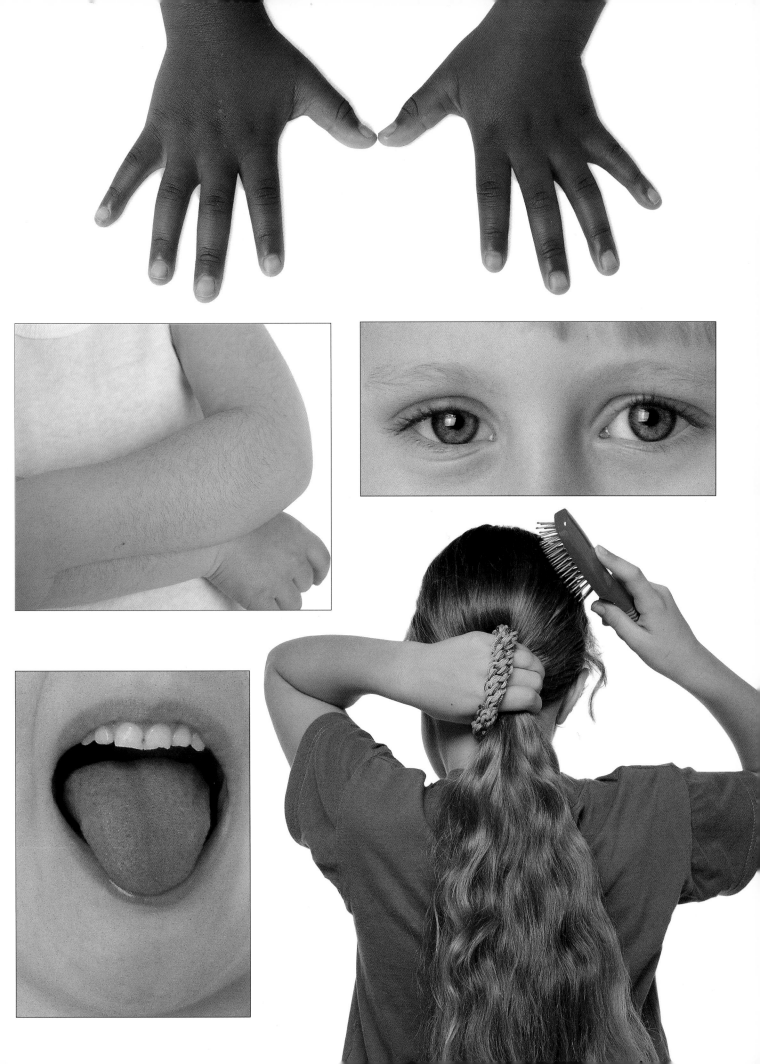

My Day

Waking Up

It's seven o'clock.
It's time to wake up.

Wake up,
teddy.

Wake up,
everyone.

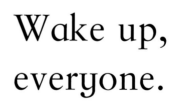

I'm awake.

I'm awake.

We're awake.

I'm awake.

Getting Dressed

It's eight o'clock.
It's time to get
dressed.

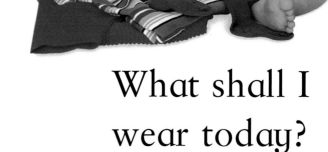

What shall I
wear today?

stripy
trousers

red T-shirt

stripy
T-shirt

blue
jumper
and blue
trousers

Which ones
shall I wear?

Now for
my shoes.

Having Breakfast

It's nine o'clock.
It's time for
breakfast.

I'm having
milk for
breakfast.

I'm having
cereal.

I'm having
toast and
jam.

orange
juice

bowls

apple juice

cup

Yum, that
was good.

yogurt

Painting

It's ten o'clock.
It's time to have some fun.

We're painting.

Do you like my painting?

paintbox

crayons

We're
drawing.

I can
paint too.

Going to the Park

It's eleven o'clock.
It's time to go to the park.

At the park
I can skip
with my
rope.

Teddy likes
skipping
too.

Wheee! Down
the slide!

It's fun on
the swing.

Teddy likes
the swing too.

Teddy likes to
ride on my bike.

Party Time

It's twelve o'clock.
It's time to go to
a party.

party
hat

presents

What's
in here?

balloon

What a mess!

Lunch

It's one o'clock.
It's lunchtime.

Let's make
lunch.

I'm having
yogurt.

I'm
eating
pizza.

What's for dessert?

ice
cream

fruit

I've
got ice
cream...

or shall
I eat an
apple?

Playtime

It's two o'clock.
Let's play.

I'm building
a big palace.

I'm building
a tower.

Oh no...

Tea Party

It's three o'clock.
Teatime for toys.

We're having
a tea party.

More
cake,
teddy?

We like
strawberries...

and jelly...

and cakes.

More tea,
teddy?

Reading

It's four
o'clock.

Big sister is back
from school.

Let's read
a book.

Teddies like to hear stories.

Do you want to read, teddy?

I'm reading too.

So am I.

Supper Time

It's five o'clock.
Time for supper.

We're eating
pizza.

We're eating spaghetti.

What a mess!

Bath Time

It's six o'clock.
Time to have a bath.

ducks

Splash!

I've got toys
and bubbles
in my bath.

I'm washing
my hair...

and cleaning
my face.

Time to
dry off.

Bedtime

It's seven o'clock.
It's time for bed.

We're in our
pyjamas.

I'm going
to brush
my teeth.

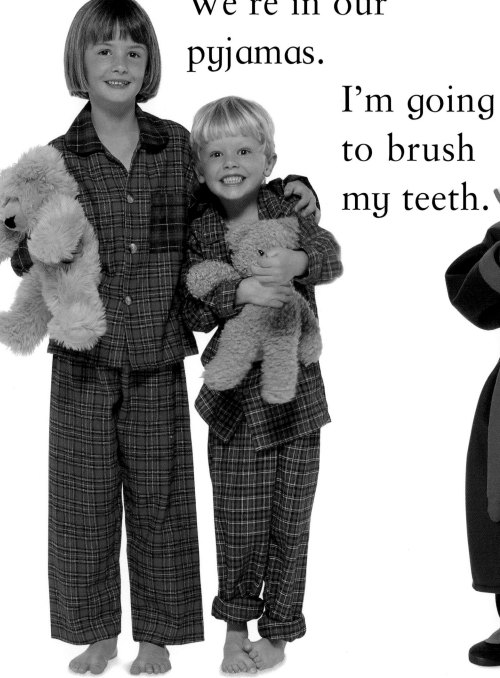

Here's a
snack.

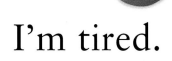

I'm tired.

Everyone's asleep.

What time is it?

Is it playtime?

Is it lunchtime?

Is it time to get up?

Is it time for bed?

Is it five
o'clock?

Is it one
o'clock?

Is it eleven
o'clock?

Is it two
o'clock?

Is it nine
o'clock?

Is it six
o'clock?

Is it three
o'clock?

Is it seven
o'clock?

Is it twelve
o'clock?

My Home

The Kitchen

Food is stored and cooked in the kitchen.

vegetables

colander

cooker

oven glove

saucepans

rubbish bin

rolling pin

apron

wooden spoons

lemon squeezer

fish slice

ladle

knives

frying pan

Fridge

Some foods need to be kept cold to stay fresh.

Look at all this food. It needs to go in the fridge.

butter

yogurt

cheese

sardines

chicken

milk

Freezer

Some foods have to be kept frozen. They go in the freezer.

fish fingers

ice

oven chips

ice cream

peas

Cooking

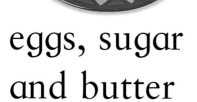

Food is cooked in the kitchen.

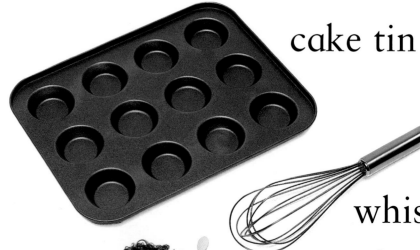

cake tin

whisk

eggs, sugar
and butter

baking
tray

We are
making cakes.

What a mess!

Cleaning Up

There are lots of things to help us clean the kitchen.

tea towel

brush

scourer

washing-up liquid

cloth

I'm drying up.

mop

bucket

Cupboard

Glasses, plates and food are kept in the cupboard.

jars

tins

bottles

biscuit tin

I'll put this away.

carton

tea caddy

cups

mugs

bowls

plates

saucers

glasses

I'm carrying glasses.

The Dining Room

The dining room is a special place for eating meals.

water jug

spoon

knife

fork

napkin

Eating lunch together.

We're hungry.

bread board

bread

fruit

What's for lunch?

place mat

Baby's Room

Sometimes babies sleep in a room of their own.

teddy

mobile

cot

I'm awake!

bottle

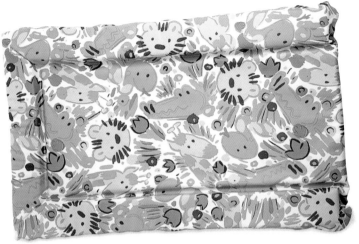

changing mat

blanket

It's
playtime.

nappy

wipes

sleeping
bag

The Bathroom

toy
boats

The bathroom is where
we wash ourselves.

toothpaste

towel

toothbrush

hairbrush

soap

duck

mirror

I'm nice
and
clean.

bath

toilet

shampoo

toilet
paper

potty

The Sitting Room

The sitting room is a comfortable place to relax.

coffee table

rug

bookshelves

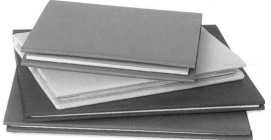

story books

table
lamp

potted
plant

cushion

bean bag

photograph

pretty
flowers

The Playroom

You can paint, draw or play with your toys in a playroom.

jigsaw puzzle

rag doll

coloured pencils

paintbox

rocking horse

tipper truck

playhouse

tea set

coat hooks

train set

hand puppet

chalk

I'm playing on my own.

The Bedroom

The bedroom is where you go to sleep and get dressed.

bookshelves

toys

clock

dressing gowns

slippers

pyjama case

chair

bin

coat hanger

Sleep tight!

In the Garden

Lots of people grow flowers in the garden.

seeds

soil

trowel

garden wire

watering can

broom

I'm gardening.

Watering
the plants.

wheelbarrow

flowerpots

Picking
flowers.

flowers

The Toolshed

The toolshed is full of tools for grown-ups to use in the home.

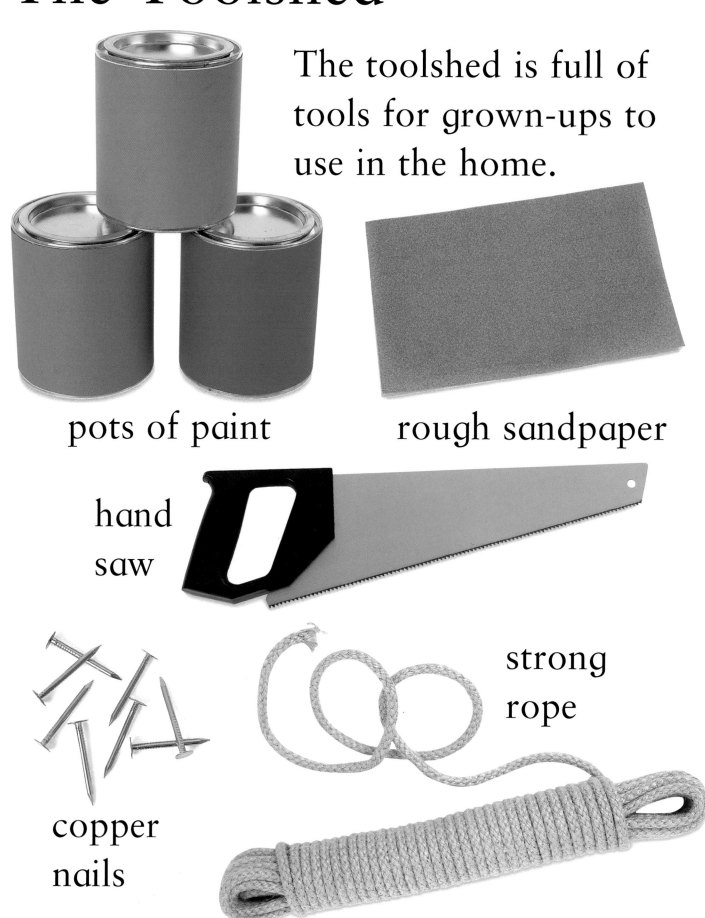

pots of paint

rough sandpaper

hand saw

copper nails

strong rope

silver
nails

screwdriver

hammer

nut

bolts

Fixing things
with toy
tools.

step
ladder

Tidying Up

There are lots of things to help us tidy up our home.

Watch out!

What a mess!

I'll help.

Where do I start?

dustpan
and brush

feather
duster

broom

That's
better.

Where do they go?

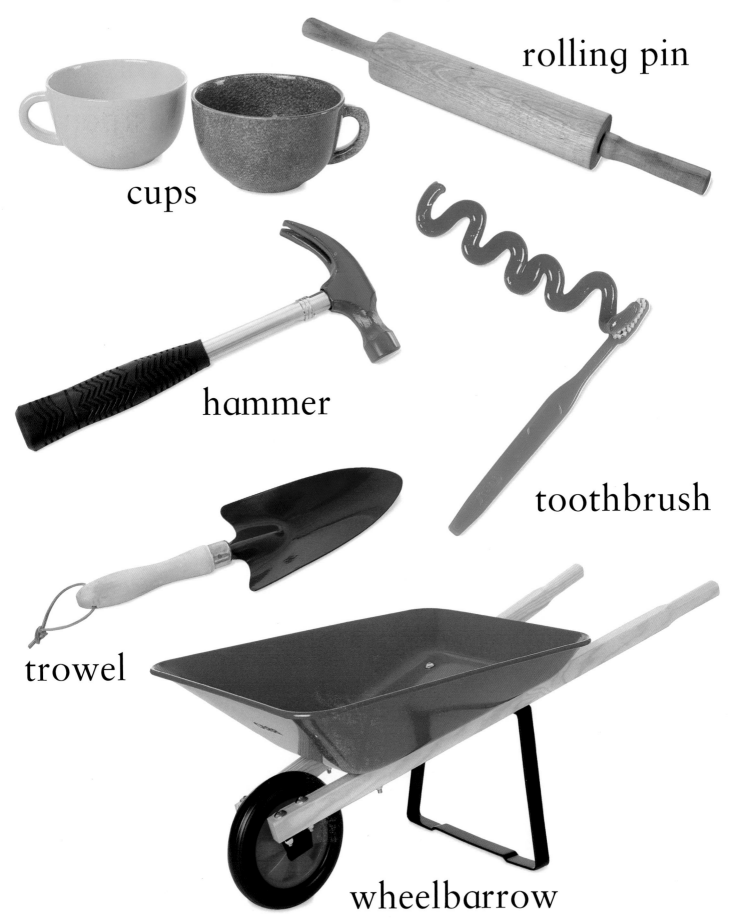

cups

rolling pin

hammer

toothbrush

trowel

wheelbarrow

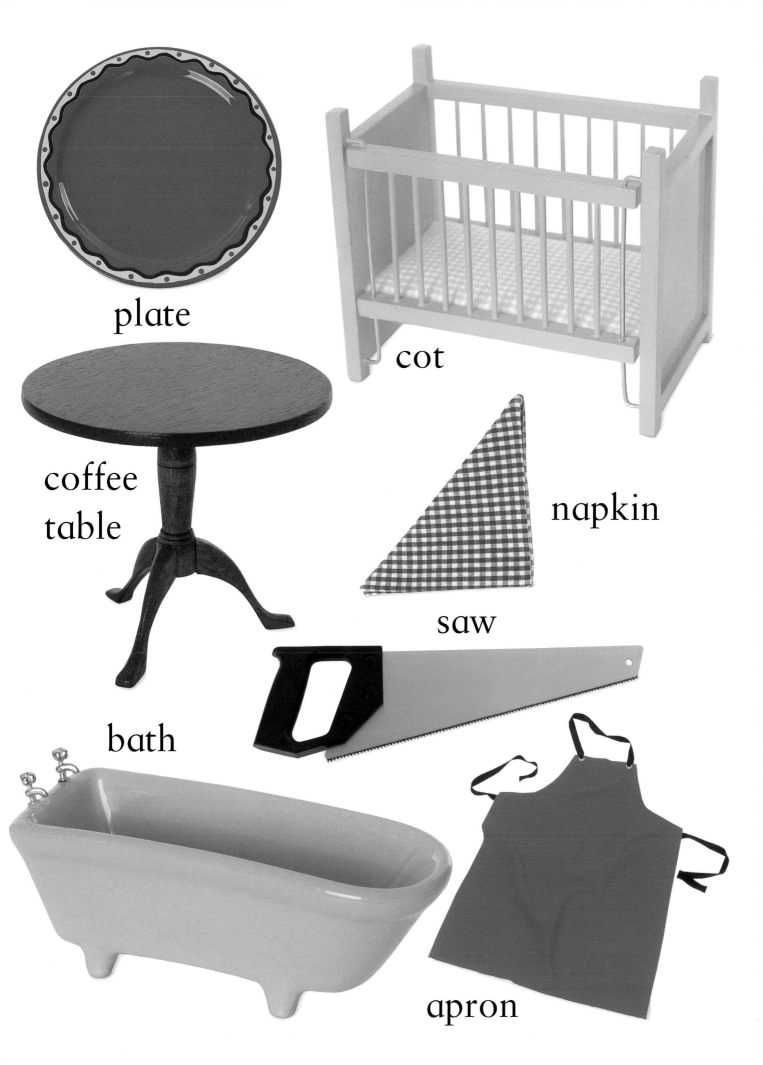

plate

cot

coffee table

napkin

saw

bath

apron

Acknowledgements

The publishers would like to thank the following children for modelling for this series of books:

Rosie Anness, Daisy Bartel, Harriet Bartholomew, Jonathan Bartholomew, Chilli Bernstein, Caspian Broad, Karl Bolger, Lee Bolger, April Cain, Milo Clare, Tayah Ettienne, Matthew Ferguson, Africa George, Safari George, Saffron George, Jamie Grant, Faye Harrison, Zoe Harrison, Jack Harvey-Holt, Max Harvey-Holt, Erin Hoel, Alice Jenkins, Kathleen Jenkins, Becky Johnson, Zamour Johnson, Rebekah Murrell, Amber McLaren, Nell Nixon, Tiffani Ogilvie, Giovanni Sipiano, Guiseppe Sipiano and Ella Wilks-Harper.